FOR
LOVE
OF HER

FOR LOVE OF HER

POEMS BY
EMILY DICKINSON

DRAWINGS BY
WALTER STEIN

Clarkson N. Potter, Inc./Publishers   NEW YORK
DISTRIBUTED BY CROWN PUBLISHERS, INC.

ACKNOWLEDGMENTS

We would like to thank Little, Brown and Co. and Harvard University Press for permission to reprint these poems. Without their kind cooperation this volume would not have been possible.

The poems are reprinted by permission of the publishers and the Trustees of Amherst College from Thomas H. Johnson, Editor, *The Poems of Emily Dickinson,* Cambridge, Mass.: The Belknap Press of Harvard University Press, copyright 1951, 1955, by the President and Fellows of Harvard College; and by permission of Little, Brown and Co.

For Sally, who selected these poems
with me, who could have written
many of them; for whom love and
concern and perfection matter.
I measure the distance.

INTRODUCTION

Pleasure, Pain, Love, and Creativity: in that order the subjects of Emily Dickinson's poetry revealed themselves to me and absorbed me, leading me in their endless pursuit. It was as though a life (mine? hers?) unfolded itself inevitably and inexorably in miniature, from youth to maturity, from innocence to wisdom.

I was first attracted by the easy poems—those about landscapes, insects, flowers, and the delight and relish with which she observed her environment. I gladly shared her pleasures.

But then her preoccupation with pain and agony and loneliness and death gripped me and brought me down with her to face reality. Afterward, her concern with love and creativity helped me climb up.

All: a passage from being affected by external stimuli to a searching for inner strength; from an aesthetic orientation to an ethical one.

Why did I choose to do a picture to go along with an Emily Dickinson poem? I like to think for the same reason that she might have written a poem to go along with a picture of mine were she alive today. She surely was fulfilled when she found the correct word, the exact phrase to express herself. For that successful creative search is perhaps answer enough to the unanswerable "whys?"

I respond to stimuli, to suggestions. And so at first there were obvious subjects: bees, clover, a dandelion, butterflies. But this was easy, and was only a fraction of the content of Emily Dickinson's poetry. Concern with pain and agony, loneliness and death was a reminder not to be mindless, not to be satisfied with making merely felicitous images, but to use what talent I had to discover symbols and metaphors that might communicate in pictures what she communicated in words with such economy and intensity. In searching for symbols I was able to think: What is pain? Nothing beautiful certainly. But something attractive inheres in the symbol one finds. And a gratifying catharsis takes place in the doing.

I could not "illustrate" these poems of hers. I could only find visual metaphors for them. And there are many poems that are beautiful and difficult for which I have made no drawings. They stand by themselves. But that Emily Dickinson was able so to convince me of her genuineness that I could make a drawing for a poem of hers is but my compliment to her genius. The anguish and hurt, the joy and delight she felt, I feel too. As I grow older and see a loved one die, or read of Emily Dickinson's agony, I too perceive reality and preoccupy myself with truth. I, too, must torture myself with moral and ethical considerations that come out of formulating unanswerable questions and knowing of our mortality.

What were the last words that Emily Dickinson spoke? What was the last poem she wrote? I like to think they had to do with love and creativity: the ultimate reason for being of her life. And so I have made drawings for some love poems too.

Throughout all my drawings, I hope there is that delicacy and gentleness that characterized Emily Dickinson herself. Also, I hope, a tenderness that is akin to (the graphic equivalent of) love. I have done drawings both in black and white and in color, the black and white reflective of her preference for incisive brevity, the color of her extravagant abandon, and all created with an awareness of her kind of careful observation as well as her manner of distillation after long contemplation.

A last question remains: Why conjoin drawing and poem? Do the drawings add another dimension to the poems? For those visually oriented, yes. For those not visually oriented—but how could they not be! Emily Dickinson was. I give you these drawings hoping that their accompaniment to the text will add dimension and variety, familiarity and surprise to the reader's experience.

Emily Dickinson's poems can stand by themselves. My drawings can stand alone, too. But together they—poem and drawing—testify to the reality of each other's existence. And my drawings respond to Emily Dickinson's line from her "Letter to the World," her plea with regards nature and herself:

> *For love of Her – Sweet – countrymen –*
> *Judge tenderly – of Me*

I heard a Fly buzz – when I died –
The Stillness in the Room
Was like the Stillness in the Air –
Between the Heaves of Storm –

The Eyes around – had wrung them dry –
And Breaths were gathering firm
For that last Onset – when the King
Be witnessed – in the Room –

I willed my Keepsakes – Signed away
What portion of me be
Assignable – and then it was
There interposed a Fly –

With Blue – uncertain stumbling Buzz –
Between the light – and me –
And then the Windows failed – and then
I could not see to see –

Our share of night to bear –
Our share of morning –
Our blank in bliss to fill
Our blank in scorning –

Here a star, and there a star,
Some lose their way!
Here a mist, and there a mist,
Afterwards – Day!

Till Death – is narrow Loving –
The scantest Heart extant
Will hold you till your privilege
Of Finiteness – be spent –

But He whose loss procures you
Such destitution that
Your Life too abject for itself
Thenceforward imitate –

Until – Resemblance perfect –
Yourself, for His pursuit
Delight of Nature – abdicate –
Exhibit Love – somewhat –

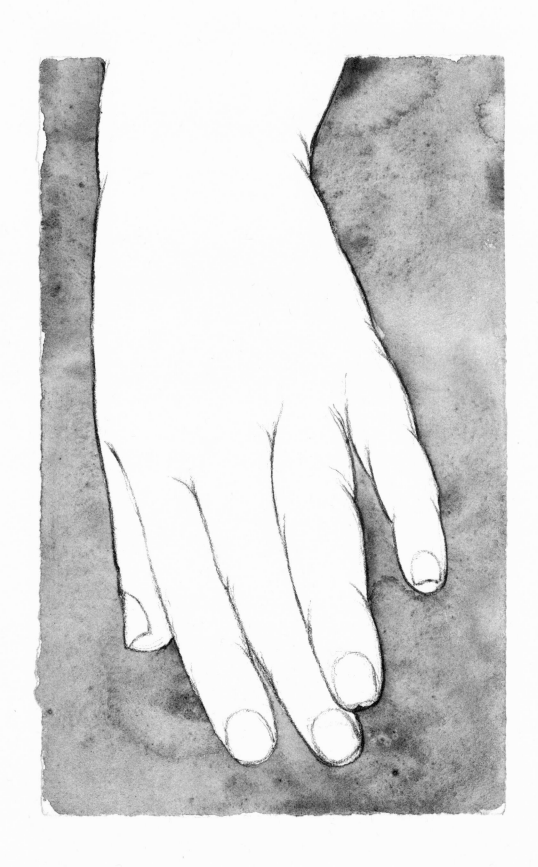

A little Madness in the Spring
Is wholesome even for the King,
But God be with the Clown –

Who ponders this tremendous scene –
This whole Experiment of Green –
As if it were his own!

After great pain, a formal feeling comes –
The Nerves sit ceremonious, like Tombs –
The stiff Heart questions was it He, that bore,
And Yesterday, or Centuries before?

The Feet, mechanical, go round –
Of Ground, or Air, or Ought –
A Wooden way
Regardless grown,
A Quartz contentment, like a stone –

This is the Hour of Lead –
Remembered, if outlived,
As Freezing persons, recollect the Snow –
First – Chill – then Stupor – then the letting go –

I reason, Earth is short –
And Anguish – absolute –
And many hurt,
But, what of that?

I reason, we could die –
The best Vitality
Cannot excel Decay,
But, what of that?

I reason, that in Heaven –
Somehow, it will be even –
Some new Equation, given –
But, what of that?

There is a pain – so utter –
It swallows substance up –
Then covers the Abyss with Trance –
So Memory can step
Around – across – upon it –
As one within a Swoon –
Goes safely – where an open eye –
Would drop Him – Bone by Bone.

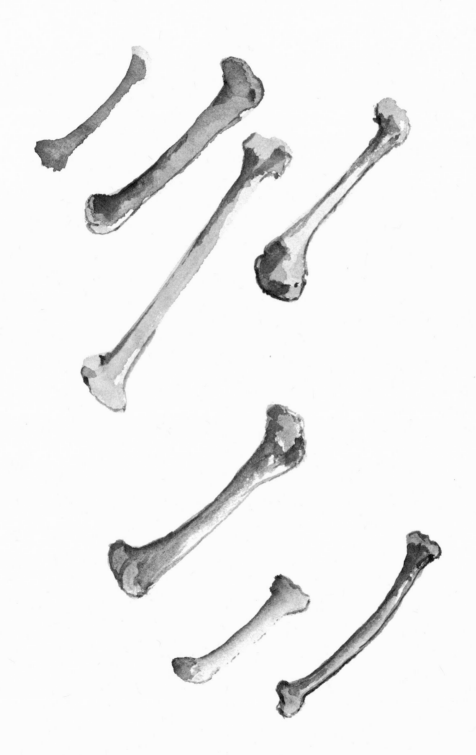

Some things that fly there be –
Birds – Hours – the Bumblebee –
Of these no Elegy.

Some things that stay there be –
Grief – Hills – Eternity –
Nor this behooveth me.

There are that resting, rise.
Can I expound the skies?
How still the Riddle lies!

The Months have ends – the Years – a knot –
No Power can untie
To stretch a little further
A Skein of Misery –

The Earth lays back these tired lives
In her mysterious Drawers –
Too tenderly, that any doubt
An ultimate Repose –

The manner of the Children –
Who weary of the Day –
Themself – the noisy Plaything
They cannot put away –

These are the days when Birds come back –
A very few – a Bird or two –
To take a backward look.

These are the days when skies resume
The old – old sophistries of June –
A blue and gold mistake.

Oh fraud that cannot cheat the Bee –
Almost thy plausibility
Induces my belief.

Till ranks of seeds their witness bear –
And softly thro' the altered air
Hurries a timid leaf.

Oh Sacrament of summer days,
Oh Last Communion in the Haze –
Permit a child to join.

Thy sacred emblems to partake –
Thy consecrated bread to take
And thine immortal wine!

The Clover's simple Fame
Remembered of the Cow –
Is better than enameled Realms
Of notability.
Renown perceives itself
And that degrades the Flower –
The Daisy that has looked behind
Has compromised its power –

If I shouldn't be alive
When the Robins come,
Give the one in Red Cravat,
A Memorial crumb.

If I couldn't thank you,
Being fast asleep,
You will know I'm trying
With my Granite lip!

Bee! I'm expecting you!
Was saying Yesterday
To Somebody you know
That you were due –

The Frogs got Home last Week –
Are settled, and at work –
Birds, mostly back –
The Clover warm and thick –

You'll get my Letter by
The seventeenth; Reply
Or better, be with me –
Yours, Fly.

Its little Ether Hood
Doth sit upon its Head –
The millinery supple
Of the sagacious God –

Till when it slip away
A nothing at a time –
And Dandelion's Drama
Expires in a stem.

Alter! When the Hills do –
Falter! When the Sun
Question if His Glory
Be the Perfect One –

Surfeit! When the Daffodil
Doth of the Dew –
Even as Herself – Sir –
I will – of You –

The Heart asks Pleasure – first –
And then – Excuse from Pain –
And then – those little Anodynes
That deaden suffering –

And then – to go to sleep –
And then – if it should be
The will of its Inquisitor
The privilege to die –

Not probable – The barest Chance –
A smile too few – a word too much
And far from Heaven as the Rest –
The Soul so close on Paradise –

What if the Bird from journey far –
Confused by Sweets – as Mortals – are –
Forget the secret of His wing
And perish – but a Bough between –
Oh, Groping feet –
Oh Phantom Queen!

Of Course – I prayed –
And did God Care?
He cared as much as on the Air
A Bird – had stamped her foot –
And cried "Give Me" –
My Reason – Life –
I had not had – but for Yourself –
'Twere better Charity
To leave me in the Atom's Tomb –
Merry, and Nought, and gay, and numb –
Than this smart Misery.

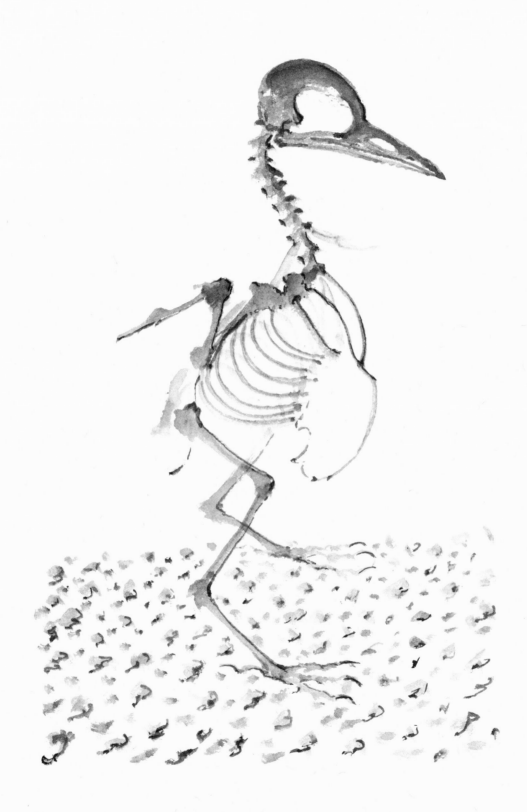

My Cocoon tightens – Colors tease –
I'm feeling for the Air –
A dim capacity for Wings
Demeans the Dress I wear –

A power of Butterfly must be –
The Aptitude to fly
Meadows of Majesty implies
And easy Sweeps of Sky –

So I must baffle at the Hint
And cipher at the Sign
And make much blunder, if at last
I take the clue divine –

That I did always love
I bring thee Proof
That till I loved
I never lived – Enough –

That I shall love alway –
I argue thee
That love is life –
And life hath Immortality –

This – dost thou doubt – Sweet –
Then have I
Nothing to show
But Calvary –

'Tis not that Dying hurts us so –
'Tis Living – hurts us more –
But Dying – is a different way –
A Kind behind the Door –

The Southern Custom – of the Bird –
That ere the Frosts are due –
Accepts a better Latitude –
We – are the Birds – that stay.

The Shiverers round Farmers' doors –
For whose reluctant Crumb –
We stipulate – till pitying Snows
Persuade our Feathers Home.

There is a solitude of space
A solitude of sea
A solitude of death, but these
Society shall be
Compared with that profounder site
That polar privacy
A soul admitted to itself –
Finite infinity.

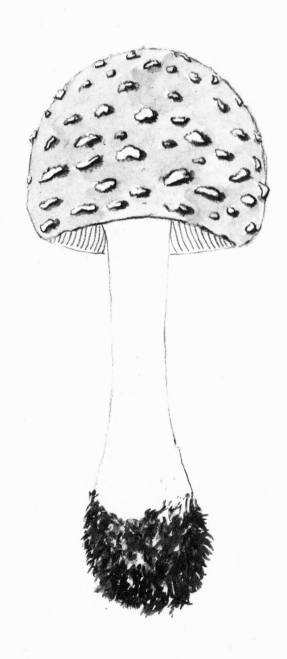

Two Butterflies went out at Noon –
And waltzed upon a Farm –
Then stepped straight through the Firmament
And rested, on a Beam –

And then – together bore away
Upon a shining Sea –
Though never yet, in any Port –
Their coming, mentioned – be –

If spoken by the distant Bird –
If met in Ether Sea
By Frigate, or by Merchantman –
No notice – was – to me –

It's easy to invent a Life –
God does it – every Day –
Creation – but the Gambol
Of His Authority –

It's easy to efface it –
The thrifty Deity
Could scarce afford Eternity
To Spontaneity –

The Perished Patterns murmur –
But His Perturbless Plan
Proceed – inserting Here – a Sun –
There – leaving out a Man –

To die – takes just a little while –
They say it doesn't hurt –
It's only fainter – by degrees –
And then – it's out of sight –

A darker Ribbon – for a Day –
A Crape upon the Hat –
And then the pretty sunshine comes –
And helps us to forget –

The absent – mystic – creature –
That but for love of us –
Had gone to sleep – that soundest time –
Without the weariness –

Too few the mornings be,
Too scant the nights.
No lodging can be had
For the delights
That come to earth to stay,
But no apartment find
And ride away.

I shall keep singing!
Birds will pass me
On their way to Yellower Climes –
Each – with a Robin's expectation –
I – with my Redbreast –
And my Rhymes –

Late – when I take my place in summer –
But – I shall bring a fuller tune –
Vespers – are sweeter than Matins – Signor –
Morning – only the seed of Noon –

A Route of Evanescence
With a revolving Wheel –
A Resonance of Emerald –
A Rush of Cochineal –
And every Blossom on the Bush
Adjusts its tumbled Head –
The mail from Tunis, probably,
An easy Morning's Ride –

If all the griefs I am to have
Would only come today,
I am so happy I believe
They'd laugh and run away.

If all the joys I am to have
Would only come today,
They could not be so big as this
That happens to me now.

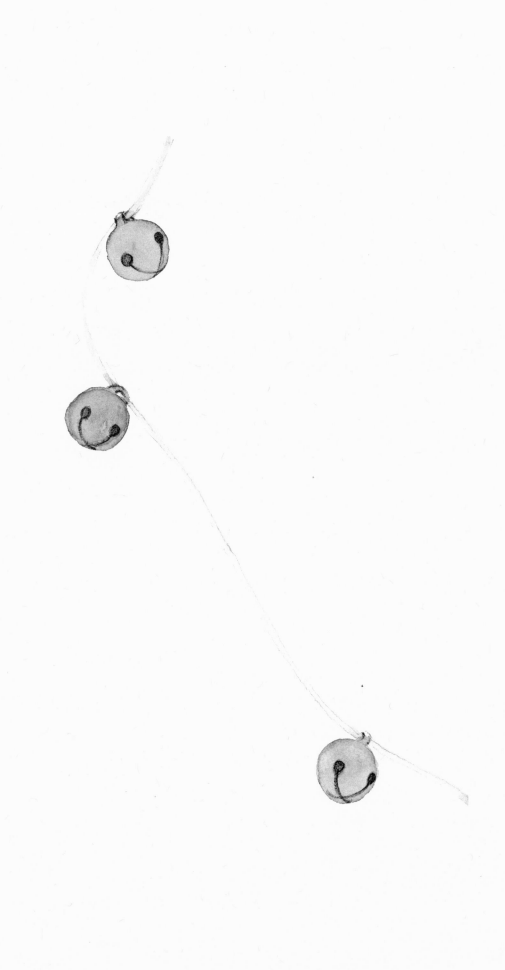

'Twould ease – a Butterfly –
Elate – a Bee –
Thou'rt neither –
Neither – thy capacity –

But, Blossom, were I,
I would rather be
Thy moment
Than a Bee's Eternity –

Content of fading
Is enough for me –
Fade I unto Divinity –

And Dying – Lifetime –
Ample as the Eye –
Her least attention raise on me –

I have no Life but this –
To lead it here –
Nor any Death – but lest
Dispelled from there –

Nor tie to Earths to come –
Nor Action new –
Except through this extent –
The Realm of you –

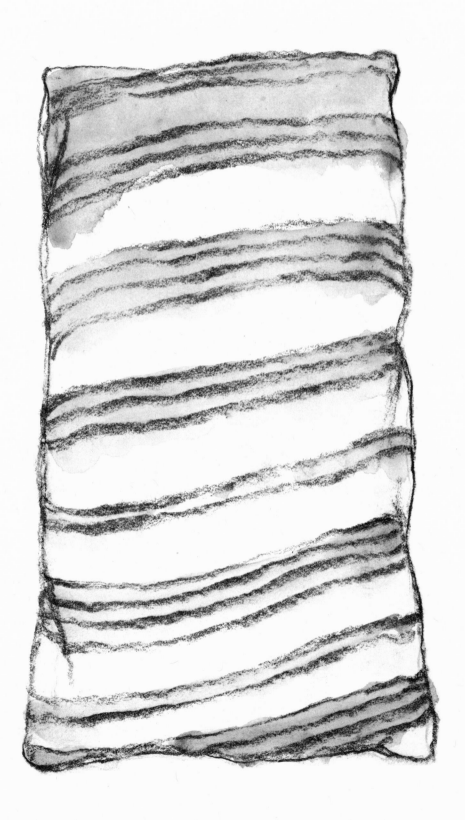

We learn in the Retreating
How vast an one
Was recently among us –
A Perished Sun

Endear in the departure
How doubly more
Than all the Golden presence
It was – before –

INDEX